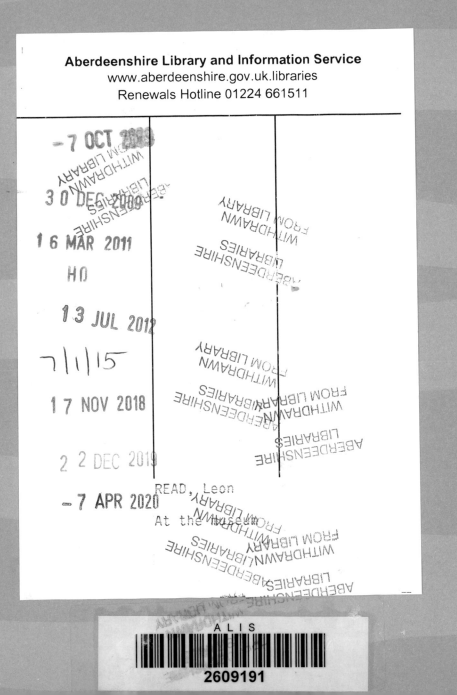

At the Museum

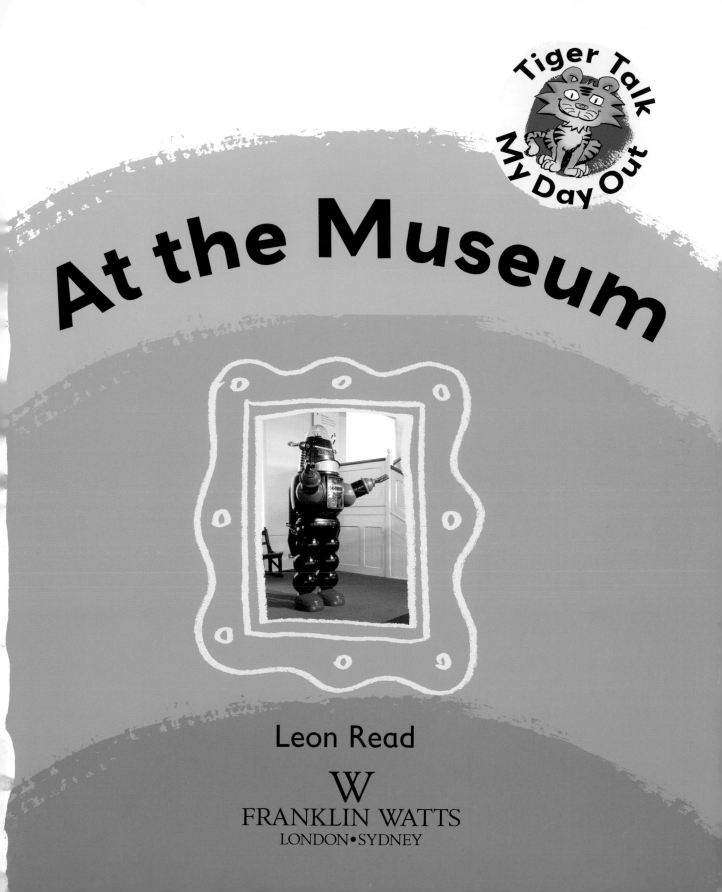

Leon Read

W
FRANKLIN WATTS
LONDON • SYDNEY

Contents

Look out for Tiger on the pages of this book. Sometimes he is hiding.

Today, Ben is going to visit the museum with his mum and sister.

Getting ready

Ben and his sister get ready.

First they have breakfast.

Then Ben helps to make a packed lunch.

Ben puts the lunch and a camera into a bag.

sandwiches

yoghurts

bananas

camera

biscuits

What else do you do before you go out?

5

Getting there

They walk to the bus stop.

The bus takes them to the museum.

What do you press to stop the bus?

The museum

This is the Museum of Childhood.

I want to see the toys.

Have you ever been to a museum? What did you see?

The museum has lots of old toys, clothes and other things on display.

Dressing up

There are lots of things to do at the museum.

← Playing outside

who will I be?
what we wear ⇨
How we learn

In the 'what we wear' area Ben and his sister dress up as firefighters.

FIRE

Now they are monsters!

This hat is too big.

What would you like to dress up as?

Sandpit play

Ben and his sister find a sandpit.

I'm moving sand with this spade.

What can you do with a bucket?

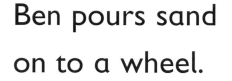

Ben pours sand
on to a wheel.

Ben! I've
got sand in
my shoe.

Then they watch
Rabbit and Tiger
put on a show.

Around the museum

After lunch, they look at some of the displays.

14

Wow! This machine really moves.

Springs and Cogs
The Wave Machine, 1980

You can set the waves in motion by placing a coin in the slot. When the motor is activated it drives a turning rod attached to a series of cams. This causes the waves to rise and fall. The waves are lifted at intervals, making them appear to ripple as they go up and down.

This automaton was made by Peter Markey (born 1930). He began making wave machines in 1980. He is fascinated by the idea of trying to produce wave-like movements from wood. It is a simple, but effective mechanism. He was inspired by the motion of a see-saw.

This machine was donated to the Museum by ... and Judith Goodison.

Tiger finds some old puppets on display.

Making things

Ben and his sister make pictures.

They draw around their hands.

Later they make models
with plastic bricks.

I am
making a
fire engine.

What would you
make with plastic
bricks?

17

Time to go

Before they go, Ben takes some photographs with the camera.

Hey, Robot! Say cheese!

I like this car.

Now it is time to go home.

My scrapbook

After their day out, Ben's mum prints out the photographs.

Ben makes a scrapbook to record the things he saw.

My favourite thing is this robot

Sunbeam racer car, 1927.

Sunbeam racer car, 1927
The real car, driven by Major Henry Segrave, reached an official land speed record of 203.792 mph. This model was made in the USA by the Kingsbury Manufacturing Co.

There were lots of clothes at the museum.

Museum website

At home Ben and his sister look at the museum website.

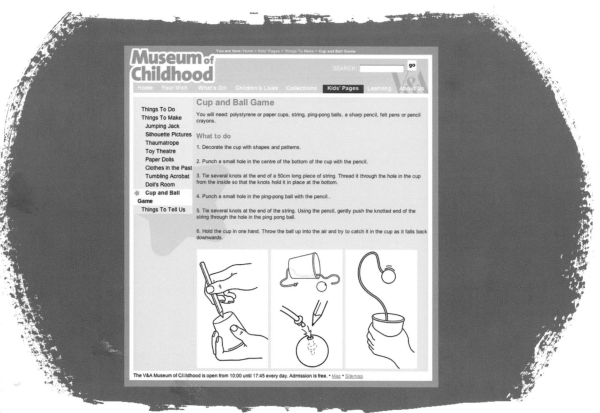

There are things to make and do.

Visit the museum website at:
www.vam.ac.uk/moc/kids

Ben prints out some sheets from the website.

They colour in the clothes.

These clothes are nearly 200 years old.

23

Word picture bank

Camera – P. 5, 18

Dressing up – P. 10

Puppets – P. 15

Robot – P. 18, 20

Sand pit – P. 12

Website – P. 22

First published in 2008 by Franklin Watts
338 Euston Road, London NW1 3BH

Franklin Watts Australia
Level 17/207 Kent Street, Sydney NSW 2000

Copyright © Franklin Watts 2008

Series editor: Adrian Cole
Photographer: Andy Crawford (unless otherwise credited)
Design: Sphere Design Associates
Art director: Jonathan Hair
Consultants: Prue Goodwin and Karina Law

A CIP catalogue record for this book is available
from the British Library.

ISBN: 978 0 7496 7623 0

Dewey Classification: 069

Acknowledgements:
The Publisher would like to thank Norrie Carr model agency.
'Tiger' and 'Rabbit' puppets used with kind permission from
Ravensden PLC (www.ravensden.co.uk).
Tiger Talk logo drawn by Kevin Hopgood.

Website screen image and printouts © V&A Museum of
Childhood (22–23). Chris Fairclough (7b).

Every attempt has been made to clear copyright.
Should there be any inadvertent omission please
apply to the publisher for rectification.

Printed in China

Franklin Watts is a division
of Hachette Children's Books,
an Hachette Livre UK company.

There are 19 Tigers, including me, in this book. Did you find all of us?

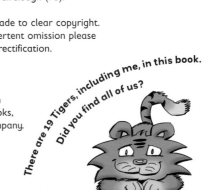